The Official
MANCHESTER CITY
Annual 2013

GW00642728

Edited by David Clayton,
Designed by Simon Thorley
Staff writer: Daniel Morehead
Dedication: Oliver Parkman

A Grange Publication

© 2012. Published by Grange Communications Ltd., Edinburgh,
under licence from Manchester City Football Club. Printed in the EU.

Photographs © PA Photos and Manchester City Football Club.

ISBN no. 978-1-908925-09-1

£7.99

Contents

Roberto Mancini

**Welcome to the Official
Manchester City Annual 2013!**

The 2012/13 season promises to be even more exciting than last year and it goes without saying we will be doing everything in our power to retain the Premier League title. We finally managed to catch our breath over the summer after the amazing last game against QPR – I still can't believe those last few minutes, though I had confidence in my team even when we were 2-1 down. I have a magnificent squad and they never gave up – these are qualities of champions and will be important for us again this season.

Of course, we will hope to do well in the Champions League as well – we did OK last year and were unfortunate to go out at the group stage, especially as we had ten points – this season we will look to progress beyond the group stage and with the final at Wembley, it's a great incentive for all the English clubs taking part.

I would also like to thank all our incredible fans for the amazing support we had last year – we won the title for you because you deserve the very best.

I hope you enjoy this Annual and remember, to achieve your dreams you need to work hard at school, eat well and listen to your parents, teachers and, if you want to be a player one day, your coach.

**See you at the Etihad Stadium,
Roberto**

Premier League Champions!

Memories are made of this! Fantastic scenes at the Etihad as the Blues celebrate a first League title for 44 years…

Victorious!

City beat Chelsea at Villa Park in the Charity Shield, the first time the Club has had the silverware since 1972

NSORED BY **McDonald's**

NNERS

ParadeofChamps!#1

More than 100,000 turned out to celebrate the Blues title success – here are some moments from what was a fantastic bus ride around Manchester city centre...

ParadeofChamps!#2

Deansgate is virtually at a standstill as the Blue buses crawl their way though the heart of city centre Manchester.
Images that will never be forgotten!

THE MOST...

What a season the 2011/12 campaign was – here are the players who, according to the stats, topped the various lists...

ASSISTS:

David Silva – 15

Nobody made more goals than City's Spanish magician with 15 to his name last season!

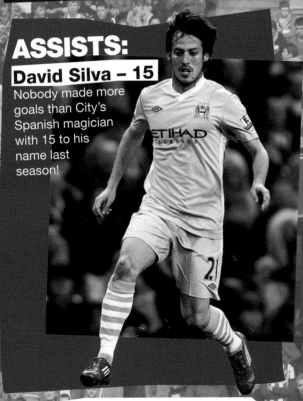

SHOTS:

Sergio Aguero – 130

Just imagine if half of Sergio's shots had gone in? He'd have scored 65 goals in his first year with the Blues!

CLEAN SHEETS:

Joe Hart – 17

Joe kept the most clean sheets of any Premier League keeper – for the second year running!

GOALS:

Sergio Aguero – 23

With 23 Premier League goals and 30 in all competitions, no wonder the brilliant Argentine won the Player of the Year Award!

BOOKINGS:

Gareth Barry – 8

Gareth clocked up the most bookings last season as our most combative midfielder.

TACKLES:

Gareth Barry – 85

No wonder Gareth got the most bookings – he made the most tackles last season!

PASSES COMPLETED:

Yaya Toure – 90.5%

With 2,189 passes completed from 2,419 attempted, the brilliant Ivory Coast star was at the heart of everything good City did last season – his amazingly successful passing rate shows why!

GAMES:

Joe Hart – 38

Joe played every Premier League game for City – the only player who could boast an ever-present League record.

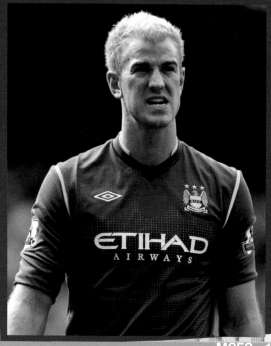

TOP TEN AGUERO CRACKERS

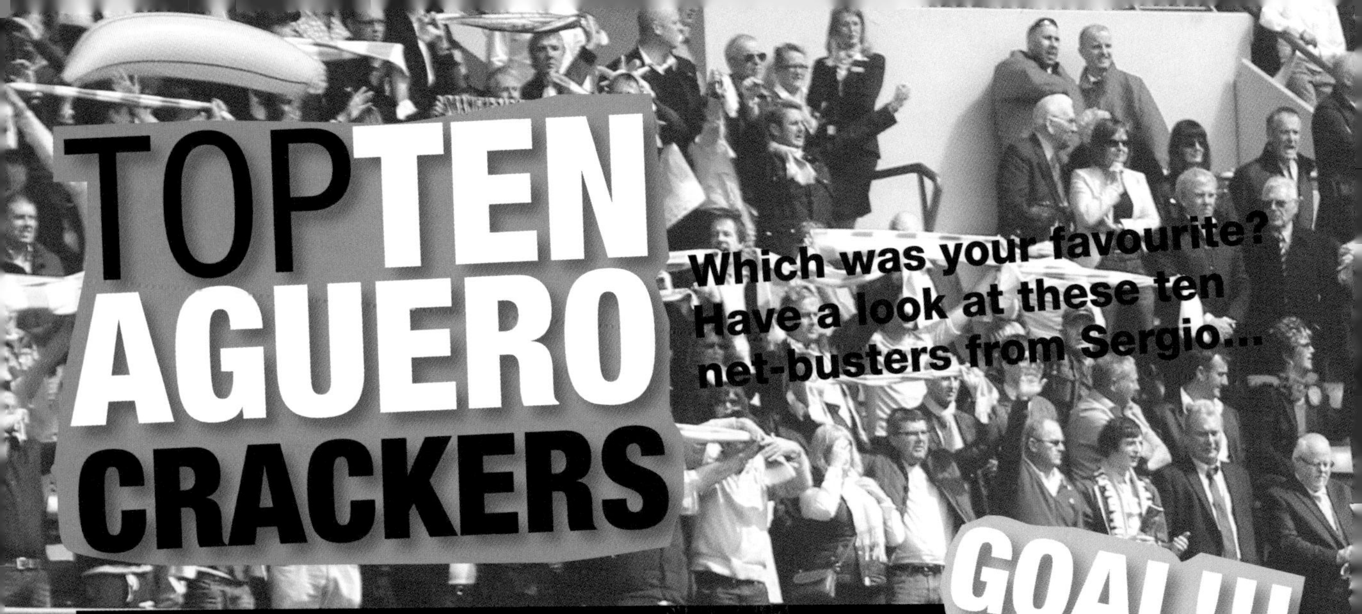

Which was your favourite? Have a look at these ten net-busters from Sergio...

GOAL!!!

03 JANUARY – LIVERPOOL

GOAL!!! A dipping shot from outside the area rifled under Liverpool goalkeeper Pepe Reina to send the Blues on the way to a blistering 3-0 win over the League Cup winners.

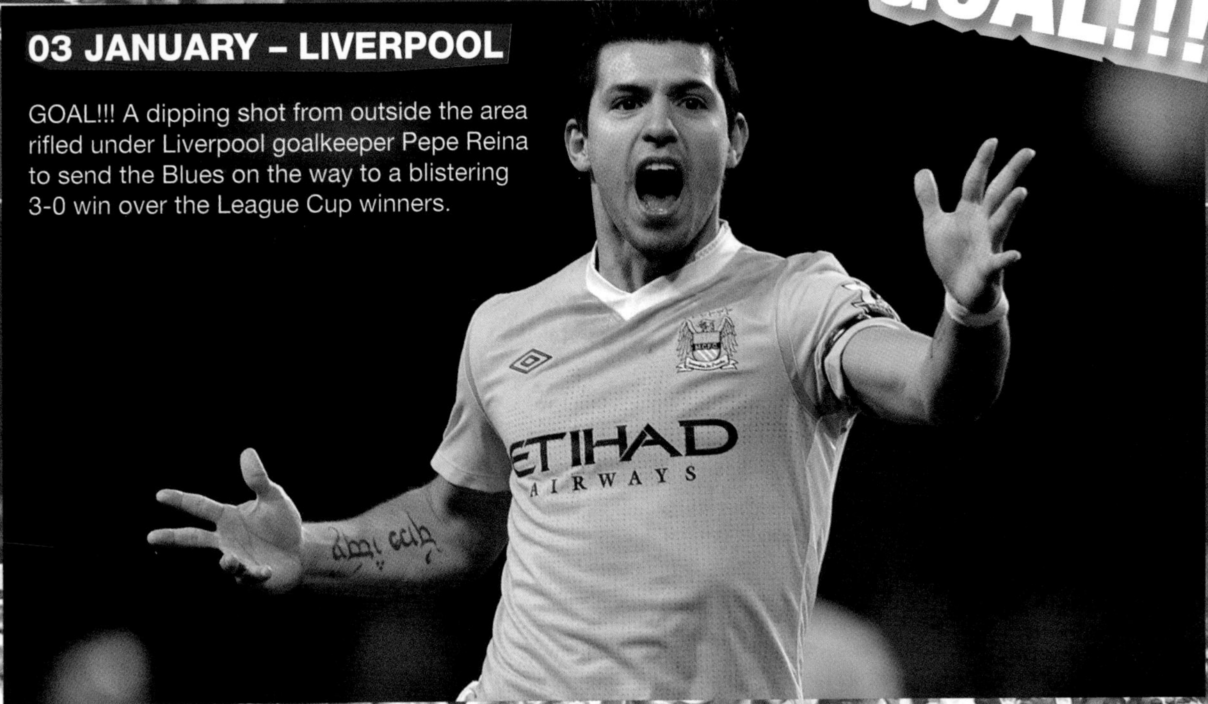

GOAL!!!

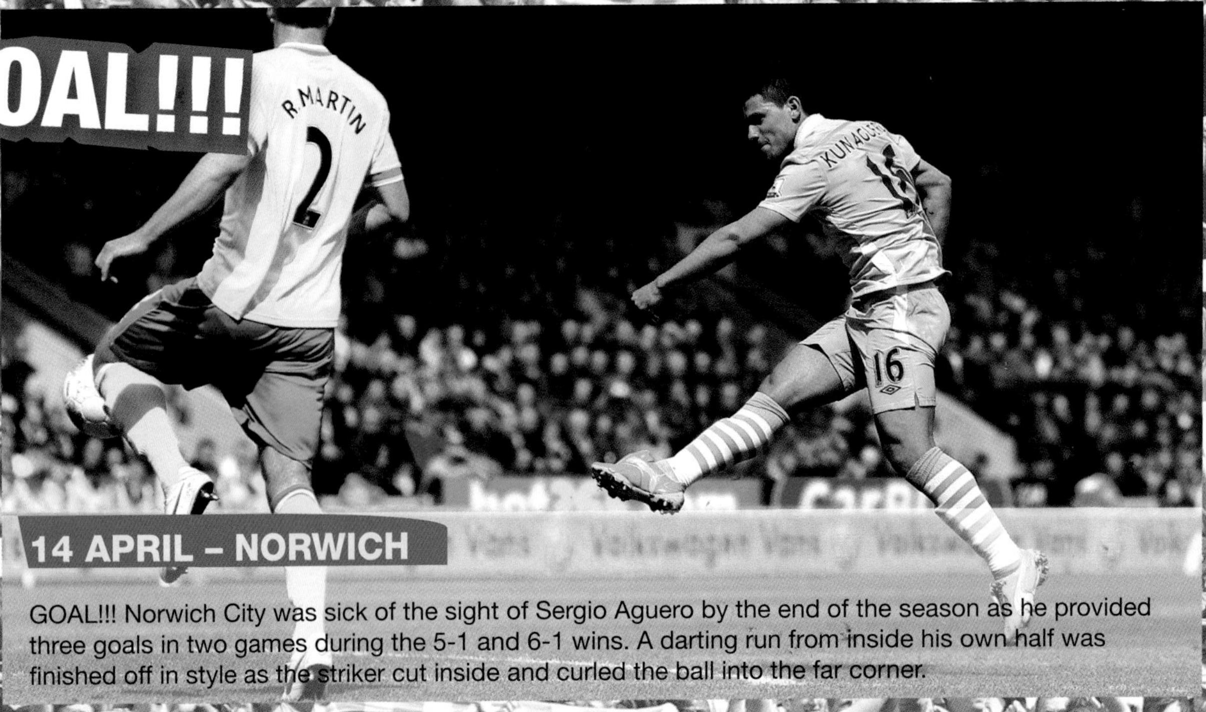

14 APRIL – NORWICH

GOAL!!! Norwich City was sick of the sight of Sergio Aguero by the end of the season as he provided three goals in two games during the 5-1 and 6-1 wins. A darting run from inside his own half was finished off in style as the striker cut inside and curled the ball into the far corner.

GOAL!!!

11 APRIL – WEST BROM

GOAL!!! A goal just five minutes into the game started the fightback which would lead the Blues to title glory. Kun's goal got City back on track after being eight points adrift of leaders Manchester United at the beginning of play.

03 DECEMBER – NORWICH

GOAL!!! By the time the ball hit the back of the net, Sergio had wriggled through and forced the ball past six opposition defenders, who could barely believe what had happened!

23 OCTOBER – MAN UNITED

GOAL!!! A trademark rampaging run by Micah Richards gave Sergio a simple tap-in to put City three goals up at Old Trafford and on the way to one of the most eye-catching results of the season.

GOAL!!!

GOAL!!!

TOP TEN AGUERO CRACKERS CONTINUED

GOAL!!! You won't see many counter-attacking goals better than this. Edin Dzeko, Adam Johnson and Sergio showed that the Blues can be deadly from any situation – even defending their own corners!

GOAL!!!

GOAL!!!

28 AUGUST – TOTTENHAM HOTSPUR

GOAL!!! Michael Dawson proved to be no match for Kun as the striker raced past him with ease. A cool left-footed shot blasted past Brad Friedel and the Blues were 4-0 up at the Lane!

14 APRIL – NORWICH

GOAL!!! Tevez and Aguero's partnership was used to its full devastating effect as the Blues ran rampant at Carrow Road. The back-heel from Tevez and finish from Kun blew the floodgates wide open.

GOAL!!!

GOAL!!!

15 AUGUST – SWANSEA

It was a debut to remember for the man they call Kun as he scored within eight minutes of making his first appearance in Blue! But Sergio didn't stop there, providing an assist for Silva and walloping home a stoppage-time stunner.

GOAL!!!

13 April – QPR

GOAL!!! The goal that won the Premier League. His 30th goal for the Blues was City's 44th shot of a breath-taking final game and the excellent one-two with Mario and way he kept his cool will live in the memory for years to come.

Roberto Mancini

Wordsearch

Can you find the names of 14 City players in the wordsearch puzzle below? Remember, the words can go upwards, downwards, sideways and diagonally - good luck!

AGUERO BALOTELLI BARRY CLICHY DEJONG DZEKO HART KOLAROV KOMPANY LESCOTT MILNER RICHARDS SILVA TEVEZ

```
T K B R M T R A H Z I F
L T V S I L V A Y L H Y
G E K O N B T Z L Y S K
M T S F R E P E T K D T
O C C C V A T B A R R Y
R D L E O O L L M R A Y
E E Z I L T M O E L H N
U J F A C T T N K D C A
G O B B F H L M Z W I P
A N T M G I Y E C Q R M
K G L P M R K N C G B O
W M P L V O Z L Y Z Q K
```

Answers on page 61

DID YOU KNOW?

Think you know everything about last season? Here are some facts you may – or may not – have been aware of...

City won every game in which they scored first.

Joe Hart won the Golden Glove for the second season in a row after keeping 17 clean sheets.

City had the most players of any club in the PFA Team of the Year: Joe Hart, Vincent Kompany, David Silva, Yaya Toure.

Mario Balotelli became the first Italian to win the Premier League.

City's record of 18 wins from 19 Premier League home games is a joint record.

20 successive home wins between 5 March 2011 and 21 March 2012 is a Premier League record.

City's average possession per game was 58%.

39% of City's shots were from outside the box.

City played an average of 504 short passes, 51 long passes, 22 crosses and 8 through-balls per game.

City's average of 2.88 points per home game was the highest in Europe's five leading leagues – England, Spain, Germany, France and Italy.

City were the Premier League's leading scorers with 93 goals.

City had the League's strongest defence, conceding just 29.

City failed to score in just five league games.

It was the first time the Premier League title has ever been settled on goal difference, but the sixth time in the history of English top flight.

Vincent Kompany won the Premier League Player of the Season Award.

City scored from 15 corners – the most in the Premier League.

City had three players in the top 10 scorers chart: Aguero, Dzeko and Balotelli.

893,851 people walked through the turnstiles during the 2011/12 season.

City didn't concede in the first 25 minutes of any League game last season.

It is over a year since the Blues lost by more than a one goal margin in the League.

City did a double over half of the teams in the League.

Sunderland are the only team the Blues failed to beat last season, drawing 3-3 at home and losing 1-0 away at the Stadium of Light.

City were the only team in Europe to have beaten both Champions League finalists – Chelsea and Bayern Munich.

Edin Dzeko's equaliser versus QPR was City's 43rd shot of the game, Aguero's winner was the 44th.

City scored the most goals from outside of the penalty area.

City scored 33 more goals than the FA Cup winning season of 2010/11.

City finished 25 points above the new European Champions, Chelsea.

The black and gold colour used in the club's badge was influenced by the symbol of the Manchester bee, a connection to the industrial Revolution.

THE TOP TEN SEASON DEFINING MOMENTS

League's aren't just won by one goal – it's a chain of events that happens on and sometimes off the pitch... here are ten decisive moments we believe made all the difference.

AGUERO ARRIVES

01

City fans had to wait for Sergio Aguero to make his first appearance in sky blue, but boy, was it worth it. The new signing missed pre-season and the City faithful only got their first glimpse of their new man in Blue when he left the bench 60 minutes into the opening game of the season. Two goals (including a 25-yard screamer) and one assist later, Kun Aguero had set down the mark for a free-scoring season.

BLITZ AT THE LANE

02

It was not long ago that City and Spurs were fighting it out for fourth place and Champions League qualification, but early in the season it became apparent that the Blues were now aiming much higher. Edin Dzeko scored a perfect hat-trick (left foot, right foot, head!) and even got an extra goal to boot. Sergio Aguero scored the other as City ran out 5-1 winners at the Lane.

03

DEMOLITION DERBY

A game which will forever be known as 'the 6-1'. City hammered neighbours Manchester United in their own backyard to heavily swing goal difference in favour of the Blues. With the title eventually being settled by goal difference, it is no surprise that City came out on top after the demolition derby.

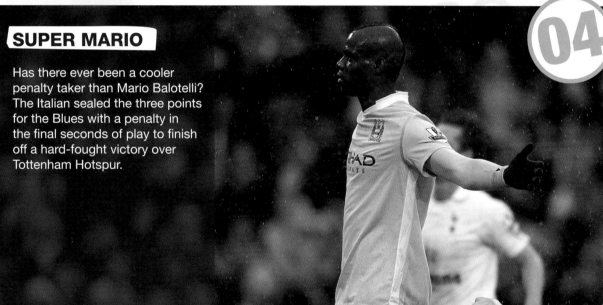

04

SUPER MARIO

Has there ever been a cooler penalty taker than Mario Balotelli? The Italian sealed the three points for the Blues with a penalty in the final seconds of play to finish off a hard-fought victory over Tottenham Hotspur.

NASRI NAILS IT

If there's one thing we learned from this season, it's the Blues like to leave it late! The scoreboard read 1-1 when Samir Nasri embarked on a darting run into the penalty area. Carlos Tevez played a clever pass back to the Frenchman who made no mistake in sending the ball past the Chelsea goalkeeper.

05

THE TOP TEN SEASON DEFINING MOMENTS

CONTINUED

06

NORFOLK KNIGHTS

The new-look strike force of Sergio Aguero and Carlos Tevez proved to be too hot for the Canaries to handle. A hat-trick for Tevez, a brace for Aguero (who can count himself unlucky to have only scored two!) and finished off by a single strike by Adam Johnson – the Blues were heading towards the title with momentum on their side.

DERBY DOUBLE

07

We all knew what had to be done. Complete a league double over United and move back to the top of the league; lose or draw and the title would most likely end up at Old Trafford. Not only did the Blues win the derby at the Etihad, they prevented their title rivals from having a single shot on target. Six points, seven goals scored and one goal conceded went a long way to bringing the Premier League trophy to Manchester.

YAYA UNLEASHED

West Brom, Wolves, Norwich and United had all fallen by the wayside as City hit form in the run-in. A tricky tie away to Champions League, chasing Newcastle United was seen by many as a stumbling block, but City confirmed their status as would-be-champions with an impressive display. Yaya Toure rampaged forward and curled a goal-of-the-season contender into the bottom corner of Tim Krul's net, then confirmed the three points with a goal in the final minute.

09

EDIN HOME

Time was counting down, hope was running out and the title was slipping out of the Club's grasp. It was only in the 91 minute that Edin Dzeko headed home a David Silva corner to level the scores and renew expectations within the stadium. It was the Bosnian's 14th league goal of the season and it is unlikely he will ever score one more important. The Blues just needed one more goal...

10

AGUER-OOOOOOO!

Be honest... how many times have you watched this? Sergio Aguero caused wild scenes of celebration with a winning goal in the 93rd minute of the final game of the season to win the first league title of the ADUG ownership. It was the Argentine's 30th goal of the season and one which will go down in history. Na na na na, na na na na, hey hey hey, Kun Aguero.

BootRoom#1 Pablo Zabaleta

Pablo Zabaleta wears Nike T90 Laser IV FG football boots.

The Spec:

The Nike Total 90 brand was first introduced in 2000. Now commonly abbreviated to T90, the range has reached its eighth generation of boots.

The Total 90 Laser IV feature a brand new dual density TPU sole plate which affords the wearer with greater traction and reducing the chance of slipping due to integrated ridges.

Contoured arch and heel support is provided by a high density EVA sock-liner. Shot power and accuracy are increased by an adaptive shield featuring plastic triangles on flexible strips. Increased ball spin is created by raised fins which create greater friction while also allowing complete control over ball accuracy.

Offering comfort and a natural ball feel, the T90 Laser IV firm ground boots are streamlined and flexible with lightweight Teijin synthetic leather upper. A larger ball-striking surface has been provided as well as a memory foam pad which increases power and accuracy.

RRP: £139.99

BootRoom#2
Joe Hart

Joe Hart wears Umbro Geometra Pro SG football Boots.

The Spec:
A memory foam 'press pad' situated on the instep assists ball control, ideal for those tricky back-pass situations. Combining modern sports technology with Umbro's football tailoring heritage, the Geometra has quickly become essential equipment. A new stud configuration is situated on the sole which allows sharp turning and greater manoeuvrability, plus a silicon-bonded grip zone for improving player touch.
Using full grain ceramic leather, a built-in sock liner and a large strike zone, the Geometra grants greater protection from any opposition challenges.

RRP: £120.00

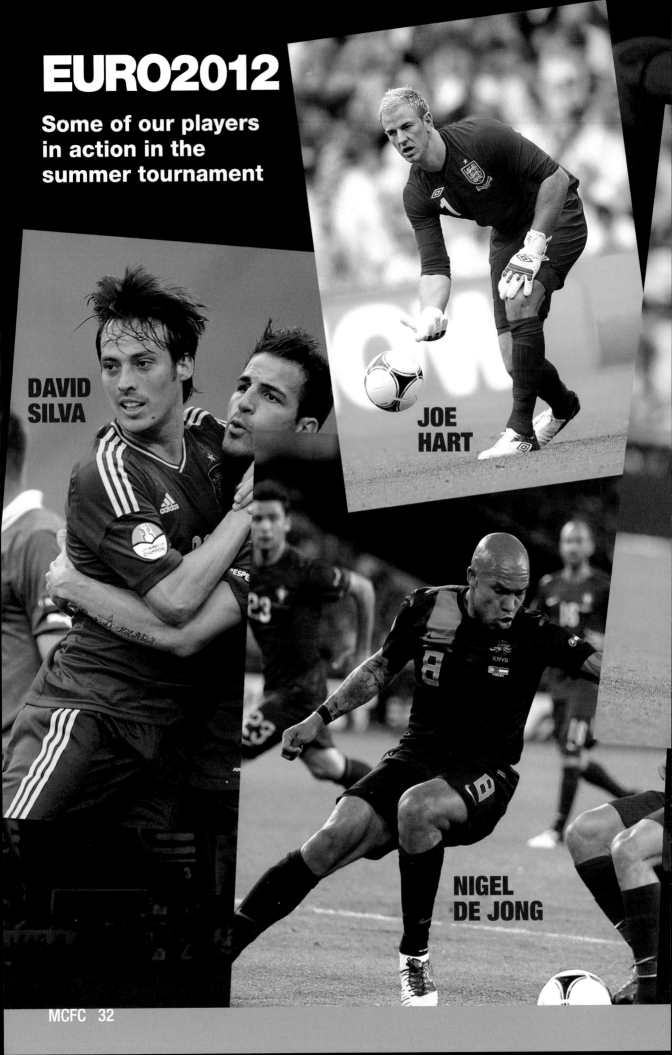

EURO2012

Some of our players in action in the summer tournament

DAVID
SILVA

JOE
HART

NIGEL
DE JONG

JOLEON
LESCOTT

MARIO
BALOTELLI

SAMIR
NASRI

Everyone loves Mario Balotelli – he's the player other football fans like the

MARIO

10 Lucky Dog?

It seems even a Premier League champion can have a soft spot for our canine friends! Mario brought a stray Labrador off the streets and into his heart and home. They are inseparable when he returns to Italy and he may soon come to live in England – paws for thought?

9 Italian International

Mario was aged just 19 years, 11 months and 29 days when he made his debut for the Italian national team. His first international goal came on 11 November 2011, surely the first of many!

8 Charity Work

Super Mario's visit to the Casa del Sole Onlus rehab centre in Mantova, Italy brought smiles to the faces of many children, with the striker even going for a ride on one of the horses used for rehab!

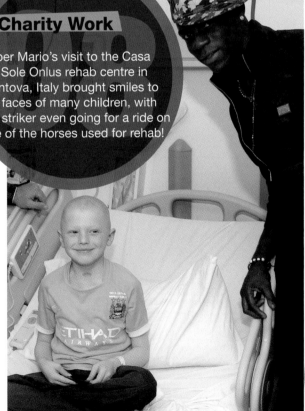

7 Golden Boy

The Golden Boy award is handed out every year to the most promising youngster in European football. Mario was awarded the 2010 prize, could he eventually go on to win the senior version, the Ballon d'Or?

6 The Bib Problem

After 30 seconds of trying (and failing!) to put on a bib during a pre-match warm up became a YouTube sensation. Even Edin Dzeko teased poor Mario about it in their next session!...

most as well as being a hero to City fans – here's Mario's top ten moments since he joined City...

BALOTELLI

5 Chicken Hat!

Television cameras caught our maverick striker wearing quite an unusual piece of headgear... a chicken hat! Reports that Mario was trying to dress like the evil penguin Feathers McGraw from the Wallace and Gromit film 'The Wrong Trousers' are so far unconfirmed...

4 Back-heel in the USA

Mario pleaded innocent after a back-heeled shot missed the target, with it being possible that he thought he was offside. His manager and mentor was less than impressed, however!

3 Head and Shoulders Above

City scored 93 league goals last season, but only Mario could score a goal quite like this against Norwich. His first shot was well saved and rather than knock in the rebound with his head, he casually shrugged the ball over the line with his shoulder!

2 Aguero Assist

Super Mario's introduction in the final game versus Queens Park Rangers provided a much-needed spark to the team. His first league assist of the season couldn't have come at a better time as he played in Aguero for the goal that won the Premier League!

1 Why Always Me?

You've most likely mimicked this celebration; you may even own a replica shirt! There is no doubt that Super Mario's number one moment in a sky blue shirt came during the 6-1 demolition derby at Old Trafford when he revealed his now famous T-shirt asking the simple question: Why always me?

Crossword

Fill the puzzle by answering the clues below

ACROSS

3 Romanian goalkeeper, Costel _____ **(10)**
5 Mario Balotelli's pet dog is called _____ **(5)**
7 Famous chant from the early 2000s.
Feed the ____ **(4)**
8 Colour of Champions League opponents
Villarreal **(6)**
10 Edison, the Uruguay striker who scored
three times v City in season 11/12 **(6)**
14 Roberto Mancini used to play for them **(9)**
17 Team Joe Hart signed for City from **(10,4)**
18 David Silva's nickname **(6)**
19 Aleksandar Kolarov's nationality **(7)**
20 Before the Etihad Stadium, the Blues
played at ____ ____ **(5,4)**

DOWN

1 The older Toure brother **(4)**
2 This Portuguese club knocked City out of
the Europa League **(8,6)**
4 Sergio Aguero's former club **(8,6)**
6 Belgian defender - not Vincent! **(6)**
9 Stadium where the Blues last lost a game
in season 11/12 **(8)**
11 Nickname of the team the Blues beat 5-2 in
the Carling Cup **(6)**
12 Vincent Kompany's nation of birth **(7)**
13 German striker for Bayern Munich who
scored three times v City in season 11/12 **(5)**
15 City mascot. Not of this world **(10)**
16 James Milner's former club **(5,5)**

Answers on page 61

Guess Who?

We've disguised four city players below - but who are they...?

Answers on page 60

Golden Silva

Here are some of the highlights of the brilliant David Silva's career so far...

Winner with Spain:

Date: 11 July 2010
Score: Netherlands 0-1 Spain (a.e.t)
Competition: FIFA WC 2010
Silva stayed on the bench as Spain claimed back-to-back major trophies. Andrés Iniesta hit an extra time winner to claim the World Cup trophy.

Date: 29 June 2008
Score: Germany 0-1 Spain
Competition: UEFA European Football Championship 2008
Spain finally fulfilled their potential as they blew away all opposition in the European Championships with their relentless tiki-taka. Silva played 66 minutes of the final before being replaced by Santi Cazorla.

Date: 24 July 2004
Score: Turkey 0-1 Spain
Competition: UEFA European Under-19 Championship 2004
A youthful Spanish side featuring Silva, current Real Madrid stars Sergio Ramos and Raul Albiol, plus Roberto Soldado and Javier Garrido claimed the prize in Switzerland.

Winner with City:

Date: 14 May 2011
Score: Manchester City 1-0 Stoke City
Competition: FA Cup 2010/11
The first trophy of the ADUG ownership was claimed at Wembley with Yaya Toure's 74th minute strike against Stoke City. Silva completed the 90 minutes as London turned Blue for the day!

Premier League 2011/12
Silva started 33 games for the eventual champions, with a further three substitute appearances. The Spaniard provided six goals and a league-high 15 assists in an impressive campaign.

Manchester City Player's Player of the Year: 2011–12
Silva's influence and popularity was obvious at the Club's End of Season awards, as he picked up the Player's Player of the Year prize.

PFA Premier League Team of The Year
Joe Hart, Kyle Walker, Vincent Kompany, Fabricio Coloccini, Leighton Baines, David Silva, Yaya Toure, Scott Parker, Gareth Bale, Robin Van Persie and Wayne Rooney made up the team voted for by every player in the Premier League.

Winner with Valencia
Date: 16 April 2008
Score: Getafe 1-3 Valencia
Competition: Copa del Rey 2007/08
Valencia claimed their seventh King's Cup victory as they triumphed in front of 54,000 at Atletico Madrid's Vicente Calderon.

Training Ground Funnies

It's not all hard work on the training ground at Carrington – the players occasionally enjoy themselves too! Here is a selection of light-hearted moments from last season...

BODY PARTS QUIZ

Test your City knowledge to the max with our Body Parts quiz – can you work out which City player is which just by looking at the body part below...?

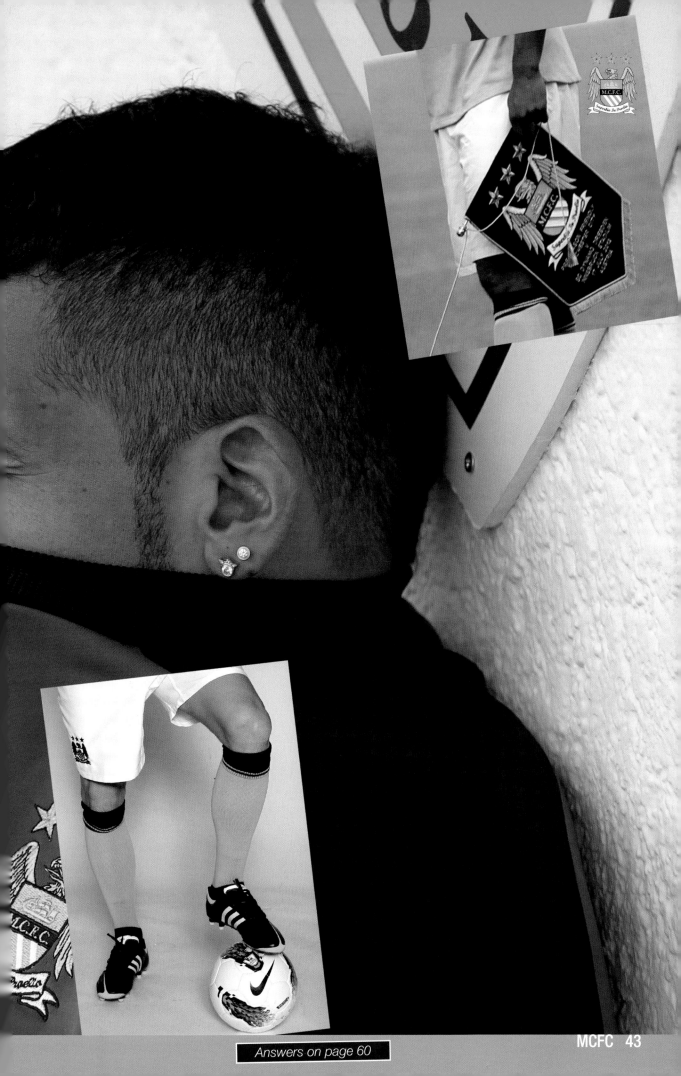

Answers on page 60

MCFC 43

New Kit Bloopers

It's a serious business, promoting the 2012/13 strip – but as City's official club photographer Sharon Latham proves – there are one or two light-hearted moments too!

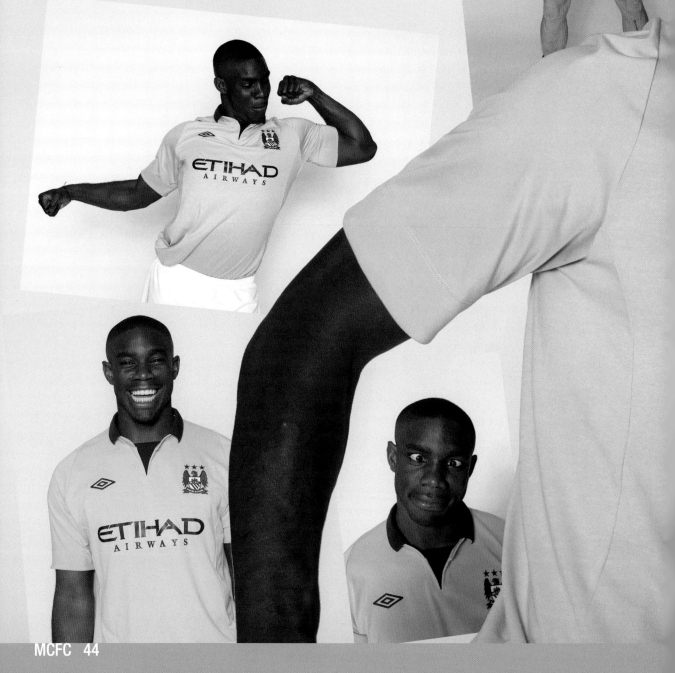

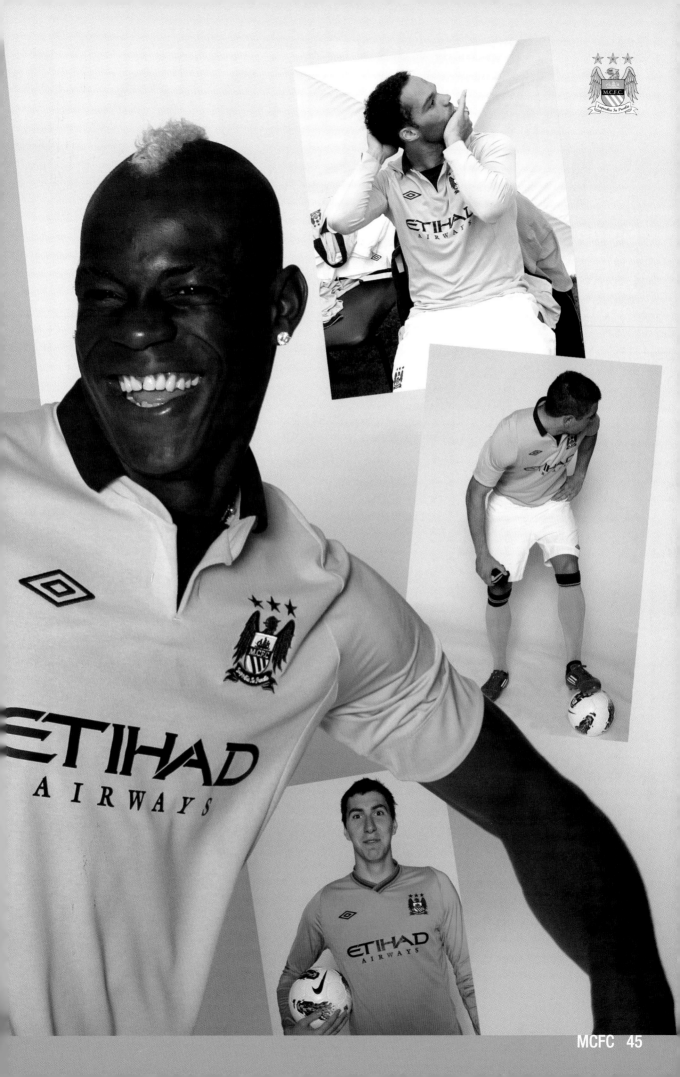

SEEN AT THE ETIHAD

Some of the stars of TV, sport and music were seen at City's home last season – did you spot any of them?

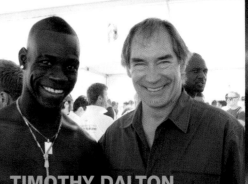

TIMOTHY DALTON

James Bond himself was at the ground in 2011 on a flying visit over from Los Angeles – another lifelong City fan, it's hardly a surprise!

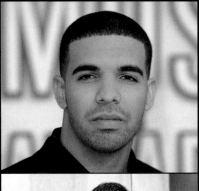

DRAKE

Canadian rap sensation Drake turned up at the Etihad to watch the Blues play Sunderland after numerous City stars had enjoyed his concert at the Manchester Evening News Arena!

LIAM GALLAGHER

The 2011/12 City kit was launched by Beady Eye and their own cover version of Blue Moon. The former Oasis man could be seen celebrating the title win during the final home game, versus Queens Park Rangers.

RICKY HATTON

Not only did the former boxer fight wearing sky blue City colours, but his entrance music was also Blue Moon! A true Blue and a regular at the Etihad.

KASABIAN (main picture)

Best-selling Leicester rockers Kasabian may be Leicester City fans, but their friendship with Liam Gallagher means they are also fond of City....

DIEGO MARADONA

One of the world's greatest footballers of all time also happens to be Sergio Aguero's father-in-law! The Argentina legend turned up to watch the Blues beat Manchester United thanks to a Vincent Kompany headed goal.

ONE DIRECTION

Again, we're not sure why One Direction came to watch the City v United clash in April – rumours they are Reds may or may not be true…

50 CENT

Though he's rumoured to be an Arsenal fan, the US rap star was spotted at the Etihad during a UK tour.

NOEL GALLAGHER

The other half of Oasis. You may have seen him interviewing Mario Balotelli in a highly entertaining feature!

SIMON COWELL

What was the X-Factor king doing watching City? We're not sure, but he asked for two tickets for the Manchester derby so who knows?

MAX, THE WANTED

A regular attendee of home games when they are not touring the world, Max is a lifelong City fan so it's not such a big surprise to see him there.

THE BIG CITY QUIZ

Do you really know all there is to know about City?
Our annual quiz will test your knowledge to the max!

1. WHO SCORED THE FIRST GOAL OF THE LEAGUE CAMPAIGN?

2. HOW MANY DIFFERENT GOALS-SCORERS DID CITY HAVE IN THE LEAGUE?
1) 15   2) 16 3) 17

3. WHICH TEAM TOOK THE MOST POINTS OFF THE BLUES?

4. NAME THE EIGHT ENGLISH PLAYERS TO PLAY FOR THE BLUES LAST SEASON?

5. NAME EVERY PLAYER TO SCORE AGAINST MANCHESTER UNITED IN THE CHARITY SHIELD, FA CUP AND PREMIER LEAGUE?

6. HOW MANY LEAGUE GOALS DID SERGIO AGUERO SCORE?
1) 23 2) 24 3) 25

7. WHO WAS THE ONLY PLAYER TO START EVERY LEAGUE GAME FOR THE BLUES?

8. WHAT NATIONALITY IS STEFAN SAVIC?

9. HOW MANY SHOTS DID THE BLUES HAVE IN THE FINAL GAME OF THE SEASON AGAINST QPR?
1) 22 2) 33 3) 44

10. HOW MANY GAMES DOES A PLAYER HAVE TO FEATURE IN TO BE ELIGIBLE FOR A LEAGUE WINNER'S MEDAL?

11. WHAT RELATION IS DIEGO MARADONA TO SERGIO AGUERO?

12. NIGEL DE JONG SCORED ONE GOAL LAST SEASON, WHO WAS IT AGAINST?

13. WHAT WAS THE BLUES TITLE-WINNING GOAL DIFFERENCE?

14. HOW MANY LEAGUE GAMES DID THE BLUES WIN?
1) 26 2) 27 3) 28

15. WHO IS THE TALLEST PLAYER IN THE CITY SQUAD?

16. WHICH CLUB WAS ROQUE SANTA CRUZ ON LOAN TO?

17. WHICH CLUB WAS THE 'POZNAN' CELEBRATION ADOPTED FROM?

18. HOW MANY RED CARDS DID THE BLUES SUFFER IN THE LEAGUE?
1) 4 2) 5 3) 6

19. HOW MANY GOALS DID CITY CONCEDE IN 19 HOME GAMES?

20. WHICH COUNTRY BEAT THE TOURES' IVORY COAST IN THE AFRICA CUP OF NATIONS?

21. HOW MANY POINTS DID THE BLUES GAIN IN THE CHAMPIONS LEAGUE GROUP STAGE?

22. WHO WON THE CLUB'S YOUNG PLAYER OF THE YEAR AWARD?

23. WHO WON THE ETIHAD PLAYER OF THE YEAR AWARD?

24. CORAZÓN DE LEÓN IS PABLO ZABALETA'S NICKNAME, BUT WHAT DOES IT MEAN?

25. HOW MANY LEAGUE TITLES HAVE THE BLUES NOW WON?

26. WHO WERE THE FIRST CHAMPIONS LEAGUE OPPONENTS AT THE ETIHAD STADIUM?

27. TRUE OR FALSE – CITY WERE THE ONLY TEAM TO BEAT BOTH CHAMPIONS LEAGUE FINALISTS?

28. WHAT WAS THE COMBINED SCORE FROM BOTH GAMES AGAINST TOTTENHAM HOTSPUR?

29. HOW MANY PREMIER LEAGUE TITLES HAS GAEL CLICHY WON?

30. WHO SCORED CITY'S FIRST-EVER CHAMPIONS LEAGUE GOAL?

Answers on page 61

MANCHESTER CITY FC
Squad Profiles 2012/13

NAME: JOE HART
POSITION: GOALKEEPER
SQUAD NUMBER: **25**

Date of Birth: 19/04/1987
Previous Clubs: Shrewsbury, Tranmere Rovers (loan), Blackpool (loan), Birmingham City (loan)

2011/12 Apps (All Comps): 52 starts
2011/12 Goals (All Comps): 0

City Career High: Justified his selection over Shay Given and cemented his place in the starting line-up on the opening day of the 2010/11 season with a man-of-the-match display at White Hart Lane.

NAME: **GAEL CLICHY**
POSITION: **LEFT-BACK**
SQUAD NUMBER: **22**

Date of Birth: 26/07/1985
Previous Clubs: Cannes, Arsenal

2011/12 Apps (All Comps): 35 starts, 1 sub
2011/12 Goals (All Comps): 0

City Career High: Won the second league title of his career as he slotted into the Premier League's leading defence.

NAME: ALEKSANDAR KOLAROV
POSITION: LEFT-BACK
SQUAD NUMBER: 13

Date of Birth: 10/11/1985
Previous Clubs: FK Cukaricki Stankom, OFK Beograd, Lazio

2011/12 Apps (All Comps): 18 starts, 7 sub
2011/12 Goals (All Comps): 4

City Career High: Scored the first-ever Champions League goal for the Blues with his late equaliser against Napoli.

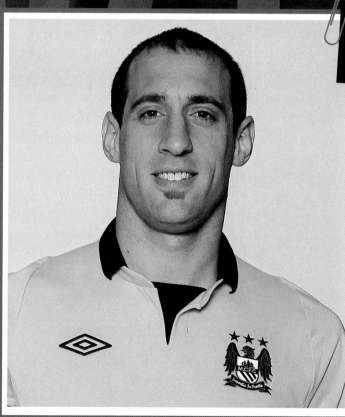

NAME: PABLO ZABALETA
POSITION: RIGHT-BACK
SQUAD NUMBER: 5

Date of Birth: 16/01/1985
Previous Clubs: San Lorenzo, Espanyol

2011/12 Apps (All Comps): 27 starts, 5 sub
2011/12 Goals (All Comps): 1

City Career High: Set the Blues on the way to the Premier League title with the opening goal versus QPR – his first, and only, goal of the season.

NAME: MICAH RICHARDS
POSITION: RIGHT-BACK
SQUAD NUMBER: 2

Date of Birth: 24/06/1988
Previous Clubs: None

2011/12 Apps (All Comps): 32 starts, 6 sub
2011/12 Goals (All Comps): 1

City Career High: Became England's youngest ever defender after impressing for the Blues in his first 28 senior appearances.

NAME: STEFAN SAVIC
POSITION: CENTRE-BACK
SQUAD NUMBER: 15

Date of Birth: 08/01/1991
Previous Clubs: FK BSK Borca, Partizan Belgrade

2011/12 Apps (All Comps): 11 starts, 7 sub
2011/12 Goals (All Comps): 1

City Career High: Opened his City scoring account with a headed effort against Blackburn Rovers at Ewood Park.

NAME: KOLO TOURE
POSITION: CENTRE-BACK
SQUAD NUMBER: 28

Date of Birth: 19/03/1981
Previous Clubs: Arsenal

2011/12 Apps (All Comps): 12 starts, 6 sub
2011/12 Goals (All Comps): 0

City Career High: Made Club captain in his first season at the club.

NAME: JOLEON LESCOTT
POSITION: CENTRE-BACK
SQUAD NUMBER: 6

Date of Birth: 16/08/1982
Previous Clubs: Wolverhampton Wanderers, Everton

2011/12 Apps (All Comps): 40 starts, 2 sub
2011/12 Goals (All Comps): 3

City Career High: Kept the Manchester United strikers so quiet that the Reds failed to attempt a single shot on target. One half of the strongest central defence in the league.

NAME: VINCENT KOMPANY
POSITION: CENTRE-BACK
SQUAD NUMBER: 4

Date of Birth: 10/04/1986
Previous Clubs: Anderlecht, Hamburger Sport-Verein

2011/12 Apps (All Comps): 41 starts
2011/12 Goals (All Comps): 3

City Career High: Scored the winning goal against Manchester United, which proved key as the Belgian went on to lift the Premier League trophy in his first season as captain.

NAME: NIGEL DE JONG
POSITION: DEFENSIVE MIDFIELD
SQUAD NUMBER: 34

Date of Birth: 30/11/1984
Previous Clubs: Ajax, Hamburger Sport-Verein

2011/12 Apps (All Comps): 23 starts, 13 sub
2011/12 Goals (All Comps): 1

City Career High: Successfully shut out Manchester United and Stoke City in the 2010/11 FA Cup Semi and Final. A tough-tackling shield in front of the defence.

NAME: GARETH BARRY
POSITION: DEFENSIVE MIDFIELD
SQUAD NUMBER: 18

Date of Birth: 23/02/1981
Previous Clubs: Aston Villa

2011/12 Apps (All Comps): 39 starts, 4 sub
2011/12 Goals (All Comps): 1

City Career High: Became a key cog inside the title-winning engine room, completing the most tackles of any City player last season.

NAME: YAYA TOURE
POSITION: CENTRAL MIDFIELD
SQUAD NUMBER: 42

Date of Birth: 13/05/1983
Previous Clubs: ASEC Mimosas, SK Beveren, Metalurg Donetsk, Olympiacos, Monaco, Barcelona

2011/12 Apps (All Comps): 41 starts, 1 sub
2011/12 Goals (All Comps): 9

City Career High: Scored the only goal of the 2010/11 FA Cup Final to win the Club a major trophy for the first time in 35 years.

NAME: JAMES MILNER
POSITION: MIDFIELD (LEFT, RIGHT, CENTRE)
SQUAD NUMBER: 7

Date of Birth: 04/01/1986
Previous Clubs: Leeds United, Swindon Town (loan), Newcastle United, Aston Villa

2011/12 Apps (All Comps): 23 starts, 14 sub
2011/12 Goals (All Comps): 3

City Career High: His typical non-stop, all-energy effort was put to great effect at Old Trafford as the Englishman's movement overloaded the United back-line.

NAME: JACK RODWELL
POSITION: DEFENSIVE MIDFIELD
SQUAD NUMBER: 17

Date of Birth: 11/03/1991
Previous Clubs: Everton

2011/12 Apps (All Comps): N/A
2011/12 Goals (All Comps): N/A

City Career High: Debut for City in 3-2 win over Southampton.

NAME: SAMIR NASRI
POSITION: ATTACKING MIDFIELD
SQUAD NUMBER: 8

Date of Birth: 26/06/1987
Previous Clubs: Marseille, Arsenal

2011/12 Apps (All Comps): 38 starts, 8 sub
2011/12 Goals (All Comps): 6

City Career High: Popped up with an 86 minute winner versus Chelsea as the Blues came from behind to keep up their spectacular home form.

NAME: DAVID SILVA
POSITION: ATTACKING MIDFIELD
SQUAD NUMBER: 21

Date of Birth: 08/01/1986
Previous Clubs: Valencia, Eibar (loan), Celta Vigo (loan)

2011/12 Apps (All Comps): 44 starts, 3 sub
2011/12 Goals (All Comps): 8

City Career High: Assisted 15 goals during the 2011/12 season, the highest in the Premier League.

MANCHESTER CITY FC
Squad Profiles 2012/13

NAME: SERGIO AGUERO
POSITION: STRIKER
SQUAD NUMBER: 16

Date of Birth: 02/06/1988
Previous Clubs: Independiente, Atlético Madrid

2011/12 Apps (All Comps): 41 starts, 9 sub
2011/12 Goals (All Comps): 30

City Career High: Scored in stoppage time against QPR to win City the league title for the first time in 44 years. His 30th goal of the season.

NAME: MARIO BALOTELLI
POSITION: STRIKER
SQUAD NUMBER: 45

Date of Birth: 12/08/1990
Previous Clubs: Lumezzane, Internazionale

2011/12 Apps (All Comps): 19 starts, 11 sub
2011/12 Goals (All Comps): 17

City Career High: *Why always me?* opened the scoring at Old Trafford in the 6-1 demolition derby.

NAME: CARLOS TEVEZ
POSITION: STRIKER
SQUAD NUMBER: **32**

Date of Birth: 05/02/1984
Previous Clubs: Boca Juniors, Corinthians, West Ham United, Manchester United

2011/12 Apps (All Comps): 7 starts, 8 sub
2011/12 Goals (All Comps): 4

City Career High: Awarded the Golden Boot for most Premier League goals after the 2010/11 season. Has scored 47 goals in 72 league games to help the Blues become the top team in England.

NAME: EDIN DZEKO
POSITION: STRIKER
SQUAD NUMBER: **10**

Date of Birth: 17/03/1986
Previous Clubs: Željeznicar, Teplice, Ústí nad Labem (loan), VfL Wolfsburg

2011/12 Apps (All Comps): 27 starts, 17 sub
2011/12 Goals (All Comps): 19

City Career High: Scored four (including a perfect hat-trick) at White Hart Lane as the Blues knocked five goals past Tottenham Hotspur.

QuizAnswers

Guess Who? (From page 37)

1 SERGIO AGUERO

2 CARLOS TEVEZ

3 PABLO ZABALETA

4 SERGIO AGUERO

Body Parts Quiz (From page 42 & 43)

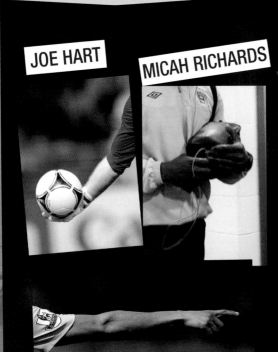

JOE HART

MICAH RICHARDS

CARLOS TEVEZ
(MAIN PIC)

VINCENT KOMPANY

GAEL CLICHY

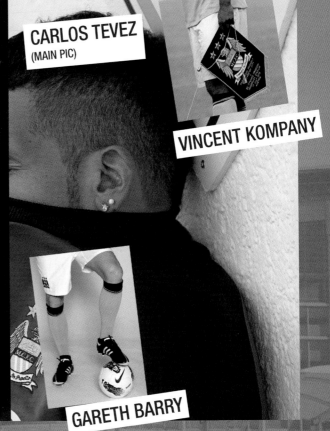

GARETH BARRY

1. EDIN DZEKO
2. 16
3. SUNDERLAND
4. JOE HART, JOLEON LESCOTT, MICAH RICHARDS, NEDUM ONUOHA, GARETH BARRY, JAMES MILNER, OWEN HARGREAVES, ADAM JOHNSON
5. VINCENT KOMPANY, ALEKSANDAR KOLAROV, SERGIO AGUERO, EDIN DZEKO, DAVID SILVA, JOLEON LESCOTT, MARIO BALOTELLI
6. 23
7. PETER CROUCH
8. MONTENEGRIN
9. 44
10. 10
11. FATHER-IN-LAW
12. LIVERPOOL
13. 64, EIGHT BETTER THAN UNITED'S 56
14. 28
15. EDIN DZEKO
16. REAL BETIS
17. LECH POZNAN
18. 5
19. 12
20. ZAMBIA
21. 10
22. DENIS SUAREZ
23. SERGIO AGUERO
24. HEART OF A LION
25. THREE
26. NAPOLI
27. TRUE! THE BLUES BEAT CHELSEA 2-1 IN THE LEAGUE ENCOUNTER AT THE ETIHAD AND BAYERN MUNICH 2-0 IN THE CHAMPIONS LEAGUE.
28. 8-3
29. TWO. ONE WITH ARSENAL'S 'INVINCIBLES, ONE WITH CITY.
30. ALEKSANDAR KOLAROV

WORDSEARCH (From page 23)

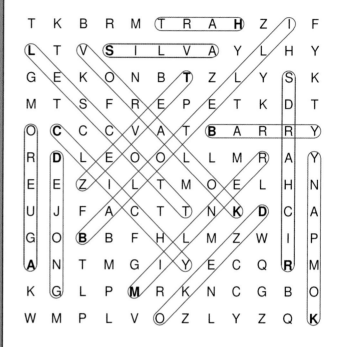

CROSSWORD SOLUTION (From page 36)

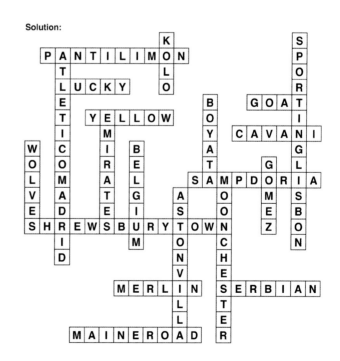

Where's Moonchester?